Home Is Where My Boys Are

Beth Bradbury

BookLeaf Publishing

India | USA | UK

Presentation by *BookLeaf Publishing*

Web: www.bookleafpub.com

E-mail: info@bookleafpub.com

ISBN: 9789357447683

First edition 2022

DEDICATION

To all my boys, my reasons for writing. I love you all so much.

Life

Life isn't easy,
No matter how hard we try.
There's always slip-ups and hiccups,
With a few disasters mixed in.
The mundane tasks in life,
Can work us to the bone.
On top of everything else,
Sometimes these things can seem impossible.
But it's ok if we let things slide,
And have a few bad days.
It's what makes us human.
We need to show our emotions,
Laugh and cry,
Sometimes bare our souls.
And some days we just hide away,
Afraid that if we let slip it might not stop,
A cascade of bubbles into a waterfall.
I hope the good times outweigh the bad,
As we muddle through life.
One thing is for sure,
And I hope it stays that way,
No matter what happens in life,
We will always have each other.

The Day I Lost Me

You see
The day I lost Me
There was you.

You see
I used to know Me when I looked in the mirror.
I haven't forgotten that flat stomach,
Now a distant memory.
Preened hair, now wild and unkempt,
I used to have the time to care.

You see
It's a shock now to me
What I look like close up.
The lines, the wobbles, the cushion tummy,
The cellulite and the size of my thighs.
The age on my face a surprise,
When did that happen?

You see
I used to know Me in my own mind.
Now my thoughts are a jumble,
Sentences blur and words get lost.
I've even lost my own name,

But it's been swapped for something far more
precious.

You see
A lot has changed.
Colleagues and friends for loneliness and long
days.
Relaxed drinks and hangovers for sleepless
nights.
Independence for reliance,
But I wouldn't change it for the world.

You see
The day I lost Me was the best day of all,
Because I got you.

Lucky

Hard days and good days, sleep finds you
eventually,
Tucked up safe, a curly haired angel.
The soft flick around your forehead,
Mouth moving gently, breathing a soft snore,
Arms flung out, beckoning a sleepy cuddle,
Oh I hope you dream happy dreams.

Guilt remembers your tears,
These toddler years bringing waves of good and
bad.
A small ask can set off a scurry of emotions,
See I forget your beautiful brain holds little
reason yet.
The red mist descends,
My judgement as clouded as yours.

I make mistakes, no matter how hard I try.
Voices rise as patience thins,
Your little face a defiant sight,
As you scream NO with all your might and fury.
Waiting out the screams without the time,
Some days it's easier to understand than others.

Your laugh, your shiny bubbly belly laugh,

Oh we have plenty of those times too.
Your eyes gleaming, dimples deep with a grin,
So wickedly clever and funny, I can't believe
you're mine.
The room lit up with joy and life all makes sense
again,
I hope this is what fills your dreams.

Your small hand as it slips in mine,
Afternoon draws in, a tired voice asking to be
held.
Your darling body fits against mine, comfort for
us both.
Just to bask in your warmth, your smell, your
love,
I wish I could hold you all day.

Sometimes it can take your breath away,
It seems strange how a love so strong can almost
cause pain.
Love doesn't seem like a big enough word,
It never wanes, only strengthens each day.
An insurmountable emotion, it can swallow you
whole.
How did I ever get lucky enough to feel it?

Second

Second time around,
Clueless to start,
But we were wiser this time.
Not as much panic,
Not as much pain,
A louder house,
A fight for attention,
But no less love.
Second to arrive
But never second best.

A beacon of light in a time of darkness,
Through fear and isolation you grew.
We kept you safe,
You knew no other,
A different experience than before.
36 weeks filled with worry,
You made it all worth it,
Another joy in our lives.
Second child,
But never second to us.

That white blonde whirl upon your head,
A sweet spot perfect to rest my lips.
Those big blue eyes gaze into mine,

The softest skin,
The warmest cradles.
One sweet hand strokes my chest in circles,
I've done this before,
But it's different with you.
Second time feeding
But not second hand magic.

My gentle little soul,
Filled with smiles and warmth,
The wonder of seeing you grow.
A laugh, a roll,
A crawl, a stand,
You do it all your own way.
A new achievement every week,
You amaze me so much.
Second to see
But never second in our eyes.

Our small bundle in an oversized sleepsuit,
Soft with baby curves.
The lightest breath in and out,
I hold mine to hear you.
The flutter of an eyelid,
The twitch of a lip,
What memories fill your head?
Maybe the arms which hold you dearly.
Second time parents
But not second hand love.

Full Cupboards

It's that time of the week again,
The cupboards are bare.
The fridge is looking sorrowful,
And in the fruit bowl sits one lonely pear.

Last nights meal was a strange concoction,
An assortment of odds and ends.
A wrinkly pepper, some leftover meat,
Mixed with a carrot that now bends.

The freezer is full of bread bags,
Crusts destined to be forgotten,
For when new loaves of bread arrive,
They'll be buried right at the bottom.

The demand for snacks is met with a grimace,
I'm sure there was a Babybel hiding.
The sad eyes of a two year old held in promise,
Brings guilty feelings about the fail of its
finding.

Everyone's surviving on cheese on toast,
Because there's always a stray chunk left.

The good butter has gone, there's only
margarine,
The suggestion which leaves us bereft.

We're obviously the lucky ones to have this
problem,
Some families have bare cupboards all year
round.
I'll do my best to raise us all thankful,
And not to pout when an apple is the only snack
left around.

See I can't deny that I'm as bad as the rest,
Sometimes only chocolate will cut it.
When the craving arises and there's none left,
After a long day, I'm just truly gutted.

But not to fret, the lure of full cupboards has
finally won,
Secretly I'm filled with glee.
I don't even mind having grumpy children in
tow,
Because it's food shop day FINALLY!

Teething Troubles

Oh your poor red cheeks,
You've had them for weeks,
With tears running from those big sad eyes,
And dribble running down onto your thighs.
Your chin is spotty from being so wet,
I wish I could help you, my poor little pet.

For is there a more sorrowful sight,
Then a teething baby, especially at night?
Why is it always worse after dark,
You were so happy today at the park.
But lay down at night, the pain truly kicks in
And my patience starts wearing thin,

With those pesky pearly whites that just won't
come.
It truly is a total pain in the bum,
For both of us, you the pain, and me the mess,
Because let me tell you, there could be less,
Soaked muslins and clothes to wash,
And those people that talk utter tosh
When they say teething can't cause explosive
nappies.
Let's just say your poor bottom isn't happy,
It's been sudocremed as much as I can manage

And I'm sure we've now got shares in Vanish.

But oh my baby what a cry,
As you look at me with those pleading eyes.
I'll dole out the calpol and hope the teething gel
numbs,
As you furiously chew things to ease those
angry gums.
But my darling if you wouldn't mind,
Taking your anger out on toys this time,
Because for the 46th time this week
Your trying to feed has been met with a shriek.
My battered nipples are cut to shreds,
And you're insistent you won't take a bottle
instead.

Some babies (parents!) get lucky and their
teething is mild,
Some get so angry and it drives others wild,
But you're just sad and it breaks my heart to see.
Plus, and I mean this in the most loving way, I
need you to sleep,
Because you're thrice nightly get ups have
quadrupled in frequency,
And I'm so TIRED, so teeth, have the decency,
To just bloody arrive, or get lost until
You're ready to come because I'm losing the
will.

The hours are so long, between midnight and 5,
And as nice as it is it see the sun rise,
A disgruntled baby and toddler the next day,
Do not make for pleasant happy play.
So note to babies, if you could consider instead,
Being born with teeth and getting ahead.
Coming out already with a full set,
Might just be a better bet!

Online Shopaholic

It's hard to decide
If shopping online
Was the best or worst invention.
Isn't it addictive,
So many offers,
Bold red writing to catch your attention.

Cramp in your thumb,
From continuous scrolling,
Fifteen websites in half an hour.
Clothes to food,
Books to shoes,
Look at that mug in the shape of a flower!

It's 3am,
The perfect time,
To buy a device for cleaning the drain.
Remember my card?
No website, no,
This affair cannot happen again.

Second hand sites,
My kryptonite,
Where I become a force to be reckoned.
Let loose on eBay,

The nail biting tension,
Bidding down to the very last second.

A burst of excitement,
When I win the item
Keeps my eyes open during late night feeds.
It's funny how they say
Breastfeeding is free,
Nobody warns of the night-time shopping
sprees.

So easy to buy,
But when it's been a bad day,
Filled with tantrums and overflowed nappies,
Then the post is delivered
And a parcel thuds through the door,
I can't deny it sure does make me happy!

Germs

Oh heck. What was that I just heard?
A first one, a second one, and then a third.
A cough, please not just a cough,
Phew, a sneeze, we can cross Covid off.

A bigger sneeze, a little red nose,
Oh now it's running, like a tiny gross hose.
You poor thing, it's the dreaded winter cold,
It's finally arrived at our little household.

Your little body droops, weak at the knees,
'Mummy, I deed a dissue' KEERCHOO you
sneeze.
Oh fun, that went directly into my eyeball,
Must add more antibac to my next shopping
haul.

Oh please don't wipe your nose on your sleeve,
You're literally holding the tissues I was sent to
retrieve.
As I feel the heat radiating off you,
I can't help but hope we avoid Daddy catching
man flu.

Let's tuck you up, a nice sofa bed,
A blanket, a drink, a cushion for your poorly
head,
Before helping your brother retreat to safer
ground.
I wonder if you'll mind a barrier of toys all
around.

It breaks my heart to see you so sick,
A good dose of Calpol should do the trick,
A set of words, we shudder at the sight,
Because Calpol means you're wide awake
through the night!

Anything but sharing my pillow, face to face,
What with all your germs, I'd appreciate my
space.
Open mouthed snoring directly into my nose,
I guess I should just be grateful you don't
dribble too I suppose.

We'll ride out the day with plenty of cuddles,
Soon you'll be back to splashing through
puddles,
And causing mischief from morning 'til noon,
I hope my darling, you feel better soon.

Tomato Pasta

When the afternoon lull has reached its peak,
And there's 2 tired children who just want to eat,
The dreaded question rears its head at me,
"Mummy I'm hungry, what's for tea?".

I'm so tired of thinking up what to cook,
Standing in front of the fridge to look.
Sometimes I need an adult just for me,
Someone to come to clean and cook tea.
I dream of a private chef of my own,
Imagine a meal service in your home!
Those tv sitcoms where they never cook a meal,
Really do hold a lot of appeal.

Mind you, even if I spend hours cooking
something nice,
We all know unless it's pizza, tomato pasta or
rice,
It's going to end up in tears and a toddler strop,
The cries of "can I have yogurt now?" echoing
none stop,
Most of the food ending up in the dog or the bin,
We should just skip tea and head straight for the
gin.

One day, I tell myself, I really will prepare.
I'll have labelled boxes, prepped with love and
care.
One for each day of the week, lunch and dinner,
Chopped and ready to cook like a total winner.
I'll be one of those Instagram mums,
Creating plates of food shaped from organic
crumbs.
A bear in a blanket from omelette and toast,
Lay in a garden of courgettes, blueberries
making a coast.

Perhaps one day, but currently the desire
Hasn't yet filled me with fire,
So once again it'll probably be,
Good old tomato pasta for tea!

An Ode to Bedtime

We've survived tea, and had a fun bath,
And cleaned and tidied the aftermath
Of a day of fun (probably laughter AND tears),
One of those days that makes Daddy want to
drink lots of beers.
Mummy drinks vodka but doesn't start 'til late,
But the need gets stronger, after eight,

Because when you should all be tucked up in
bed,
WE'RE STILL TACKLING BLOODY
BEDTIME INSTEAD.
We bought music players, comforters and
bedtime books,
But you, my darling, give zero f... ahem, ducks,

Because somehow from 4-6pm,
You're all droopy and sleepy, but after then,
You come ALIVE, the brightest little star,
The thirstiest you've been all day by far.
You all of a sudden need 1000 wees,
And you can't lie still, no matter how much we
plead.

Feet are flying everywhere and arms are
whackin',
As you toss around in your bed, loudly yackin',
How many words can one little boy say?!
My ears are bleeding, please give it a rest for
today.
You twist and tug Mummy and Daddy's hair,
Until it's wrapped around your fingers, toes, and
everywhere.
I thought your brother was the reason I was
going thin up there,
But no, it's for sure, your regime of torture on
my poor hair.

It's not all bad, occasionally,
You'll turn, ask for a cuddle and stroke my face
nicely,
And then, I'll feel so bad for getting cross,
Because sometimes, you act like you do give a
toss.
And even though you've just thumped me round
the face and laughed,
And you've done nothing but kicked and faffed,
I love you so much, with all my heart,
From your head to your toes, and even your farts
(you find them funny, what's not to love)!

Eventually, hours in,
Sleep will finally FINALLY kick in.

Your droopy lids start to close,
And your hair winding hand starts to doze.

Your breathing deepens as you start snoring,
Your ridiculous questions stop (at least until
morning).

And then, I look at you and smile,
Because you're the most beautiful thing I've
seen by miles.
Well you and your brother,
And I'm so lucky, to be your mother.
I kiss your curls and tell you I love you,
And I know that you love me too,
Because we're the most fantastic team,
You, your brother, Daddy and me.

And although bedtimes drive me up the wall,
I remember you won't always be this small,

And also Daddy does bedtimes most nights,
(Feeding your brother gets me out of the fight).

I hope you always want the chats, if not the
cuddles,
And I'm here to work through any of your
muddles.
My little boys are growing up so fast,

I'll try and treasure every second that has
passed.

But when you're yapping away so full of energy,
The kind you couldn't muster to go for a walk at
half past 3,
And it's been 2 hours since you went up to bed,
And Daddy is the only sleepyhead,
In the room that's going dark,
And on Daddy's head you've left your mark,
From where you cracked it with your foot,
And by some miracle haven't left a cut,
It's really hard to not just breathe in deep
And yell WILL YOU JUST GO THE F*** TO
SLEEP!

Grab a Brew

Is there anything
A cup of tea won't solve?
Bad day?
Tired?
Spare biscuit?
Grab a brew.
When that kettle boils,
Is there a greater sound,
Than the click of the kettle
And the water pouring over the teabag,
A proper British comfort.
We all have our favourite tea,
Tetley, PG Tips, it's always Yorkshire for me.
Heaven forbid someone buy the wrong ones,
A month follows of disappointing cuppa's.
The sight of an empty tea canister,
Can really ruin the whole day.
Is it even possible to start a day
Without a decent tea?
And let's face it,
It's the only proper way to end one too.
Cuppa's, brews, tea,
You're always there for me.
And I vow to stay loyal
To that warm hug of a favourite drink.

Bad Night

Tonight is a bad night
I'm so tired
Not just a bit tired
Bone achingly exhausted
My eyelids long to shut
My brain barely holds together a thought
Instead I sit in this chair
Feeding, rocking and shushing

The 2 year old we thought slept well
Awake and restless throughout instead
I'm glad he finds comfort in our bed
But I need him to stop pulling my hair
Tossing and turning
Stroking my arm, my face, my back
Touched out is a real thing
And I am it

Nights are hard
With the moon comes loneliness
Hours get longer
And I sit in this chair feeding and comforting
I envy Daddy sleeping soundly
It's not his fault
You just don't find comfort in him at night

But oh how I wish I could sleep again

Don't take my complaints
For a lack of love
I wouldn't swap you both for the world
But a night of sleep would help me so much
Tonight I had enough
I let you cry in your bed a little too long
And upset your brother
Even the dog told me off

I'm so sorry boys
I wish I had done better
I just needed 5 minutes alone
Sometimes it's just really really hard
You won't remember this
But I feel the weight of the guilt
I'll do better in the future
But tonight is a bad night

Look At You

You're growing so fast little one,
Time passes in a blur.
Yesterday you couldn't and now you could,
Your brain must be a whirr.

Look at you trying to roll!
Legs have mastered it but your shoulder is stuck.
You try and try and try again,
One more push and you've done it, look!

Look at you trying to crawl!
Those little arms and legs swimming,
A fish out of water, but oh how clever,
That army crawl is just the beginning.

Look at you trying to stand!
You pull yourself up, such a strong tiny body,
A big grin across your face, success!
For a first attempt, that's far from shoddy.

Look at you trying to talk!
Your mouth testing different forms,
Such power in those lungs, such potential,
Soon you'll be babbling up a storm.

You're growing so fast little one,
Flying through tasks so complex.
Yesterday you couldn't and now you could,
I wonder what you'll do next?

Age Got Me

You know you're getting on a bit,
When bedtime has arrived by 9:30pm,
And you've worn out another pair of slippers
again.
When your drink of choice is a decaf tea,
And you have to get up in the night to pee.
When you get so excited about a new mop,
Did I tell you it was HALF PRICE on my shop?!
You lust after the advert showing a carpet
cleaner,
And the thought of an evening using it just
makes you keener.
The suggestion of a night out grips you in fear,
If the organiser has left the ending time unclear.
What if it ends up being a really late one?
I feel tired already and it's not even begun.
The concept of an early night brings such a
thrill,
And you mean sleep, not 'Netflix n chill'.
You can't get up without counting first,
And being cold is the absolute worst.
You shop around for a 'nice' bottle of wine,
Instead of the cheapest that'll do at the time.
Metabolism gives up and the extra snacks stick,

But it's fine, you're down with the kids and can
call yourself 'thicc'.
You're suddenly more comfortable in your own
skin,
When you realise a lot more comes from within.
So even though your knees creak,
And at 2:30pm you need an afternoon sleep,
And basic words are suddenly hard to recall,
Maybe growing up is kind of nice after all.

Butterfly

There's something so addictive about the smell
of a newborn baby.
That tiny frail body snuggled up on your chest,
Wisps of the softest hair,
As they gently snore,
Milk dribbles gathering in their folds,
So still and content in an after feed coma.

Heads that loll, backs the size of your hand,
Dressed in clothes that have swallowed them
whole,
Rolled up in all directions.
Then you blink and they're bigger,
Stronger and more alert.
Growing before your eyes into these little
people.

Such different personalities but all with the
similar needs.
You wish time away in that colicky phase,
The first 6 months sometimes a battle
Beyond your comprehension.
It'll be ok when they get past this phase,
We say on repeat in the darkest of hours.

But then suddenly they do,
6 months arrives and a new baby emerges,
Like a butterfly out of a cocoon,
A friend instead of foe.
And you wonder where time went,
Craving that tiny baby back that needed you
always.

It seems so illogical
That you can wish time away,
Yet want it to stop at the same time.
We're nearly at a whole year now,
And already my heart is breaking,
But also bursting with excitement to see what's
ahead.

The smiliest sweetest child,
Through sickness and health,
You've had some hard phases that have nearly
broken us,
But I'd do it all again tomorrow.
Because somehow that tiny darling baby has
grown into this wonderful little boy,
Without me truly noticing.

I almost grieve the time passed,
In case I didn't treasure it enough,
And I can't wait to see the future,
What you grow up into.

But for now I'll happily stay in this moment
with you,
And take in as much as I can.

Haircut Nightmares

Getting a haircut should be a treat,
Instead, it's an hour or more
Of staring intently at yourself in the mirror,
Noticing things you never noticed before.

It starts out well, you know you'll end up
looking better,
Shake out the mop of hair and suggest a trim as
they ask,
"What are we doing with this today?",
Whilst gingerly combing through their
mammoth task.

Next comes the hair wash,
Relaxing at first, until the return to the chair.
Never before have you truly seen
How strange your face looks when framed with
wet hair.

The more you stare, the stranger you become,
You question everything you've ever known,
From the shape of your face,
To if your double chin has grown.

The more they chop, the worse it gets,
Hair being thrown in every direction.
A blast of the hairdryer just adds insult to injury.
Finally it's time to dry it section by section.

The relief rains down as the drying continues,
You become something half recognisable.
But you've made a mental note for the future,
Staring at yourself for that long was not
advisable!

One Day

It might rain today,
A heavy patter on the ground.
Skies of grey
Rolling clouds as far as the eye can see,
No refuge, just damp misery.
Maybe a rainbow will come,
Or maybe not.
Some days will mist,
A fog so thick, blinding and suffocating.
Some will bring storms,
Loud and angry, mighty crashes deafening.
Some will hail,
A brutal force, painful and cold,
But the sun will shine again.
A soft caress of light air,
Blue sky, a halo of sweet relief.
Gentle warmth bringing a whisper of happiness,
And we'll finally be able to breathe again,
One day.

Washing Pile

I don't believe it! Surely not.
That can't be a full laundry bin.
I only emptied that yesterday,
And today it's stuffed to the brim!

I'm pretty convinced that in this house
Live an extra team,
Throwing clothes in when I'm not looking,
Til the basket is busting at the seams.

Four people cannot possibly wear,
This amount of clothes,
And how do so many wet towels appear?
It's a mystery that nobody knows.

Tiny clothes and baby socks
Are the worst to wash and dry.
Sure, they're small and cute to look at,
But to hang out on the maiden oh my,

You wouldn't believe just how many
One washing load can hold.
The socks disappear down the back of radiators,
And the rest are a nightmare to fold.

Adult clothes are no better,
So heavy and big to hang about.
The windows steam up with condensation,
As the heating dries them out.

When the sun starts shining down,
It's a panic to get washing done in time,
To really get the full benefit,
Of drying 2 or 3 loads out on the line,

For a washing free house
Is the best kind of day.
When the baskets are finally empty,
And all the laundry is put away.

You can bask in the few moments,
How tidy everything looks.
Before realising it's bed changing day,
Then sigh and say "Oh f***".

Threenager

The closer you are to three,
The more attitude you're getting.
If we don't do exactly what you want,
You start screaming like a banshee.
I've heard the threenager term,
Banded about before,
And now I see exactly what they mean,
My fears have been confirmed.
I've never before known the drama,
A wrongly cut sandwich could cause,
Or the fact you could ever incorrectly peel,
A perfectly ripe banana.
Heaven forbid I suggest to you,
The wrong pair of shoes,
Or that you may wish to ride the balance bike,
You insisted on bringing along too.
I know I lose my patience more times than a
few,
When I've tried asking nicely,
Not to push your brother over,
I struggle with what else to do.
It'll be a hard learning curve these next few
years,
For you and for me.
I'll be more patient and do my best,

To understand a little more, the tears
And the frustration on your part,
As you adjust to understanding the world.
I'll try and keep a gentler approach,
And not totally lose heart.
Because nearly 3 has also brought a boy so
funny, kind and sweet
Playing games with a wild imagination
Dancing round to music, always helping
A little old man before your time with slippers
on your feet
Remember even the days you drive me mad,
You still are my dear little boy.
And even when you've had a corker,
I really hate to see you sad.
So whether I'm at the end of my tether,
Or killing it with kindness,
Whatever's going on inside that head of yours,
We'll figure it out and ride the wave together.

These Four Walls

If these four walls could talk, they'd tell a hefty
story.
Years of good times and some bad,
Love, arguments, laughter and tears.
We arrived 2 naïve young adults,
Through successes and mistakes,
We learnt a lot.
We started our family with a puppy,
Then added another one to the mix.
We grew into parents,
Bringing back two newborn babies
And watching them grow into two beautiful
people,
Navigating our way into the unknown.
They say it's just bricks and mortar,
It's the people inside that count,
But this house has kept us safe and together
Through all weathers and pandemics alike,
Littered with photographs and happy memories
throughout.
If this house could talk, I'd tell it thank you,
For being more than just a house,
For being our home.

Thank You

What would I do
Without friends and family like you.

Be it handing out moral support
As we stomp out child free on a walk,
Or at the end of a phone
Listening to my laughs and moans.
A distance between us doesn't stop
Knowledge that you're there when I need to
sound off.

Someone I can text at 2am
When we're having a sleepless night AGAIN,
Or someone to message throughout the day,
Some company from far away.
Someone who's always been there over the years
Throughout thick and thin, laughter and tears.

Friends with kids the same age as mine,
Surviving through the same times,
Taking turns to deal with the attitudes,
Sympathetic and full of gratitude,
That we have each other to understand,
The extras that come with parental demands.

Family by blood and family in law,
It's so unfair one of you drew the short straw,
But even through your own battle
You still will listen to me prattle.
A second family I'm lucky indeed
To have so many around whenever I need.

The past 2 years have been the toughest
And somehow we've got through even the
roughest
Of days, just the kids, you and me,
All tucked away in our house safely.
I'll never be able to thank you enough
For sticking with me through the messiest of
stuff.

Some days it's hard to see through the mud
And realise life is filled with love.
On the loneliest of nights or brightest of days
You're all there in your own ways.
So to you all I truly say
Thank you so much in every way.